50 Best Dessert Recipes of the Year

By: Kelly Johnson

Table of Contents

- Classic Tiramisu
- Salted Caramel Lava Cake
- Lemon Meringue Pie
- Raspberry Sorbet
- Matcha Cheesecake
- Chocolate Chip Cookie Dough Brownies
- Pistachio Baklava
- Panna Cotta with Berries
- Apple Crumble
- Red Velvet Cupcakes
- Churros with Chocolate Sauce
- Vanilla Bean Panna Cotta
- Lemon Blueberry Pound Cake
- Chocolate Soufflé
- Crème Brûlée
- Black Forest Cake
- Mocha Trifle
- Vanilla Almond Cake
- Raspberry Almond Tart
- Peanut Butter Chocolate Pie
- Pecan Praline Cheesecake
- Banana Foster Cake
- Key Lime Pie
- Coffee Hazelnut Torte
- Strawberry Shortcake
- Chocolate Dipped Strawberries
- Mango Sorbet
- Carrot Cake with Cream Cheese Frosting
- Chocolate Coconut Macaroons
- S'mores Bars
- Coconut Cream Pie
- Brown Butter Chocolate Chip Cookies
- Pumpkin Cheesecake
- Chilled Lemon Pudding
- Triple Chocolate Mousse

- Cherry Clafoutis
- Strawberry Rhubarb Galette
- Ice Cream Sandwiches
- Blueberry Lemon Cheesecake Bars
- Matcha Green Tea Cookies
- Cinnamon Roll Apple Pie
- Coconut Rice Pudding
- Chocolate Hazelnut Truffles
- Cherry Almond Cake
- Lemon Coconut Bars
- Flourless Chocolate Cake
- Almond Joy Cheesecake
- Honey Lavender Ice Cream
- Apple Cinnamon Rolls
- Passion Fruit Panna Cotta

Classic Tiramisu

Ingredients:

- 1 cup strong brewed coffee, cooled
- 1/4 cup coffee liqueur (optional)
- 3 large egg yolks
- 1/2 cup granulated sugar
- 1 cup mascarpone cheese
- 1 cup heavy cream
- 1 teaspoon vanilla extract
- 24 ladyfingers
- Unsweetened cocoa powder (for dusting)
- Dark chocolate shavings (optional)

Instructions:

1. **Prepare the coffee mixture**: In a shallow dish, combine the cooled coffee and coffee liqueur (if using). Set aside.
2. **Make the mascarpone mixture**: In a bowl, whisk together the egg yolks and sugar until light and thick. Fold in the mascarpone cheese until smooth.
3. **Whip the cream**: In another bowl, whip the heavy cream and vanilla extract until stiff peaks form. Gently fold the whipped cream into the mascarpone mixture.
4. **Assemble the tiramisu**: Briefly dip each ladyfinger into the coffee mixture (do not soak) and layer them in the bottom of a 9x13-inch dish. Spread half of the mascarpone mixture over the ladyfingers. Repeat the process with another layer of dipped ladyfingers and mascarpone mixture.
5. **Chill**: Cover and refrigerate for at least 4 hours, preferably overnight, to allow the flavors to meld.
6. **Serve**: Just before serving, dust with cocoa powder and top with chocolate shavings if desired.

Salted Caramel Lava Cake

Ingredients:

- 1/2 cup unsalted butter
- 8 oz dark chocolate, chopped
- 1/2 cup granulated sugar
- 2 large eggs
- 2 large egg yolks
- 1 teaspoon vanilla extract
- 1/4 cup all-purpose flour
- 1/4 teaspoon salt
- 1/4 cup caramel sauce (store-bought or homemade)
- Sea salt flakes for garnish

Instructions:

1. **Prepare the baking dish**: Preheat the oven to 425°F (220°C). Grease and flour 4 ramekins and set aside.
2. **Make the chocolate batter**: In a saucepan, melt the butter and dark chocolate over medium heat, stirring until smooth. Remove from heat and stir in the sugar, eggs, egg yolks, and vanilla extract until well combined.
3. **Add the dry ingredients**: Stir in the flour and salt until just combined.
4. **Assemble**: Spoon a small amount of batter into each ramekin. Add a spoonful of caramel sauce in the center, then cover with the remaining batter.
5. **Bake**: Bake for 12-14 minutes, or until the edges are set but the center is still soft.
6. **Serve**: Let the cakes sit for 2 minutes, then run a knife around the edges to release the cakes. Invert onto plates and sprinkle with sea salt. Serve warm.

Lemon Meringue Pie

Ingredients:

- **For the crust:**
    - 1 1/4 cups all-purpose flour
    - 1/2 teaspoon salt
    - 1/2 cup unsalted butter, cold and cut into pieces
    - 4-6 tablespoons ice water
- **For the filling:**
    - 1 1/2 cups water
    - 1 cup granulated sugar
    - 1/4 cup cornstarch
    - 1/2 teaspoon salt
    - 4 large egg yolks, lightly beaten
    - 1 tablespoon lemon zest
    - 1/2 cup fresh lemon juice
    - 2 tablespoons unsalted butter
- **For the meringue:**
    - 4 large egg whites
    - 1/4 teaspoon cream of tartar
    - 1/2 cup granulated sugar

Instructions:

1. **Make the crust**: Preheat the oven to 375°F (190°C). In a food processor, combine the flour and salt. Add the cold butter and pulse until the mixture resembles coarse crumbs. Gradually add the ice water and pulse until the dough forms. Roll out and fit into a 9-inch pie pan. Bake for 10-12 minutes or until golden. Let cool.
2. **Prepare the filling**: In a saucepan, combine water, sugar, cornstarch, and salt. Bring to a boil, stirring constantly, until thickened. Gradually whisk in the egg yolks, lemon zest, and lemon juice. Cook for another 2-3 minutes until thick. Remove from heat and stir in butter.
3. **Prepare the meringue**: In a bowl, beat the egg whites with cream of tartar until soft peaks form. Gradually add sugar and beat until stiff peaks form.
4. **Assemble and bake**: Pour the lemon filling into the baked crust. Spread the meringue on top, sealing the edges. Bake at 375°F (190°C) for 10-12 minutes until golden. Cool before serving.

Raspberry Sorbet

Ingredients:

- 4 cups fresh raspberries
- 1 cup water
- 1 cup granulated sugar
- 1 tablespoon lemon juice

Instructions:

1. **Make the syrup**: In a saucepan, combine the water and sugar. Bring to a boil, stirring occasionally until the sugar dissolves. Remove from heat and let cool.
2. **Puree the raspberries**: In a blender or food processor, puree the raspberries until smooth. Strain through a fine mesh sieve to remove the seeds.
3. **Combine**: Mix the raspberry puree with the cooled sugar syrup and lemon juice.
4. **Freeze**: Pour the mixture into an ice cream maker and churn according to the manufacturer's instructions. Transfer to a container and freeze for at least 4 hours before serving.

Matcha Cheesecake

Ingredients:

- 1 1/2 cups graham cracker crumbs
- 1/4 cup granulated sugar
- 1/2 cup unsalted butter, melted
- 3 (8 oz) packages cream cheese, softened
- 1 cup granulated sugar
- 1 tablespoon matcha powder
- 3 large eggs
- 1 teaspoon vanilla extract
- 1/2 cup sour cream

Instructions:

1. **Make the crust**: Preheat the oven to 325°F (165°C). Combine graham cracker crumbs, sugar, and melted butter. Press the mixture into the bottom of a 9-inch springform pan. Bake for 10 minutes and cool.
2. **Prepare the filling**: In a large bowl, beat the cream cheese and sugar until smooth. Add matcha powder and mix until fully incorporated. Add eggs one at a time, followed by the vanilla extract. Mix in the sour cream.
3. **Bake**: Pour the mixture into the cooled crust and bake for 50-60 minutes, or until the center is almost set. Turn off the oven, leave the door ajar, and let the cheesecake cool for 1 hour.
4. **Chill**: Refrigerate for at least 4 hours before serving.

Chocolate Chip Cookie Dough Brownies

Ingredients:

- **For the brownies:**
    - 1/2 cup unsalted butter
    - 1 cup granulated sugar
    - 2 large eggs
    - 1 teaspoon vanilla extract
    - 1/2 cup all-purpose flour
    - 1/3 cup unsweetened cocoa powder
    - 1/4 teaspoon salt
- **For the cookie dough layer:**
    - 1/2 cup unsalted butter, softened
    - 1/4 cup brown sugar
    - 1/4 cup granulated sugar
    - 1 teaspoon vanilla extract
    - 1 cup all-purpose flour
    - 1/2 teaspoon salt
    - 1/2 cup mini chocolate chips

Instructions:

1. **Make the brownie layer**: Preheat the oven to 350°F (175°C). Grease and flour a 9x9-inch baking pan. In a bowl, melt butter and stir in sugar, eggs, and vanilla. Add flour, cocoa powder, and salt. Mix until smooth. Pour into the prepared pan and bake for 20-25 minutes.
2. **Make the cookie dough layer**: Cream together butter, brown sugar, granulated sugar, and vanilla. Add flour and salt, then stir in chocolate chips. Once the brownies are baked and cooled slightly, spread the cookie dough over the top.
3. **Chill and serve**: Chill in the fridge for 1 hour before cutting into squares.

Pistachio Baklava

Ingredients:

- 2 cups shelled pistachios, chopped
- 1 cup walnuts, chopped
- 1 tablespoon sugar
- 1 teaspoon ground cinnamon
- 1 package phyllo dough (16 oz)
- 1 cup unsalted butter, melted
- 1 1/2 cups granulated sugar
- 1 cup water
- 1/2 cup honey
- 1 teaspoon vanilla extract

Instructions:

1. **Prepare the filling**: In a bowl, mix the pistachios, walnuts, sugar, and cinnamon.
2. **Assemble the baklava**: Preheat the oven to 350°F (175°C). Brush a 9x13-inch pan with melted butter. Layer 8 sheets of phyllo dough, brushing each with butter. Spread a thin layer of the nut mixture over the dough. Repeat with 8 more sheets of phyllo and another layer of nuts. Continue layering until all the phyllo and nut mixture are used. Finish with 8 sheets of phyllo on top.
3. **Cut and bake**: Cut the baklava into squares or diamonds. Bake for 30-35 minutes until golden.
4. **Make the syrup**: In a saucepan, combine sugar, water, and honey. Bring to a boil, then simmer for 10 minutes. Stir in vanilla extract.
5. **Drizzle syrup**: Pour the hot syrup over the baklava and let cool before serving.

Panna Cotta with Berries

Ingredients:

- 1 1/2 cups heavy cream
- 1/2 cup whole milk
- 1/4 cup granulated sugar
- 1 teaspoon vanilla extract
- 1 tablespoon gelatin powder
- 1/4 cup cold water
- Fresh berries (strawberries, raspberries, blueberries)

Instructions:

1. **Prepare the panna cotta**: In a saucepan, heat cream, milk, and sugar over medium heat until sugar dissolves. Remove from heat and stir in vanilla extract.
2. **Bloom the gelatin**: In a small bowl, sprinkle gelatin over cold water and let sit for 5 minutes. Add the gelatin mixture to the cream mixture and stir until dissolved.
3. **Chill**: Pour the panna cotta mixture into ramekins or glasses. Refrigerate for at least 4 hours.
4. **Serve**: Top with fresh berries before serving.

Apple Crumble

Ingredients:

- 6 large apples, peeled and sliced
- 1 tablespoon lemon juice
- 1/2 cup granulated sugar
- 1 teaspoon cinnamon
- 1/4 teaspoon nutmeg
- 1/2 cup all-purpose flour
- 1/3 cup rolled oats
- 1/4 cup brown sugar
- 1/4 teaspoon salt
- 1/4 cup unsalted butter, cubed

Instructions:

1. **Prepare the apples**: Preheat the oven to 350°F (175°C). In a bowl, toss the apples with lemon juice, sugar, cinnamon, and nutmeg. Spread in a greased 9x9-inch baking dish.
2. **Make the crumble topping**: In a separate bowl, mix flour, oats, brown sugar, and salt. Add butter and rub between your fingers until the mixture resembles coarse crumbs.
3. **Bake**: Sprinkle the crumble topping over the apples and bake for 40-45 minutes, or until the apples are tender and the topping is golden brown.
4. **Serve**: Serve warm with vanilla ice cream or whipped cream.

Red Velvet Cupcakes

Ingredients:

- 1 1/2 cups all-purpose flour
- 1 cup granulated sugar
- 1 teaspoon baking soda
- 1/2 teaspoon salt
- 1 tablespoon unsweetened cocoa powder
- 1 large egg
- 1/2 cup vegetable oil
- 1/2 cup buttermilk
- 1 tablespoon red food coloring
- 1 teaspoon vanilla extract
- 1 teaspoon white vinegar

For the cream cheese frosting:

- 8 oz cream cheese, softened
- 1/2 cup unsalted butter, softened
- 3-4 cups powdered sugar
- 1 teaspoon vanilla extract

Instructions:

1. **Prepare the cupcakes**: Preheat the oven to 350°F (175°C). Line a 12-cup muffin tin with cupcake liners. In a large bowl, whisk together flour, sugar, baking soda, salt, and cocoa powder. In a separate bowl, whisk the egg, oil, buttermilk, food coloring, vanilla extract, and vinegar. Add the wet ingredients to the dry ingredients and stir until smooth.
2. **Bake**: Divide the batter evenly between the cupcake liners and bake for 18-20 minutes, or until a toothpick inserted into the center comes out clean. Let the cupcakes cool completely.
3. **Make the frosting**: Beat the cream cheese and butter together until smooth. Gradually add the powdered sugar and vanilla extract, beating until fluffy.
4. **Frost the cupcakes**: Once the cupcakes have cooled, frost with the cream cheese frosting.

Churros with Chocolate Sauce

Ingredients:

- **For the churros:**
    - 1 cup water
    - 1/2 cup unsalted butter
    - 1 tablespoon granulated sugar
    - 1/4 teaspoon salt
    - 1 cup all-purpose flour
    - 2 large eggs
    - 1 teaspoon vanilla extract
    - Vegetable oil (for frying)
- **For the sugar coating:**
    - 1/2 cup granulated sugar
    - 1 teaspoon ground cinnamon
- **For the chocolate sauce:**
    - 1/2 cup heavy cream
    - 4 oz semi-sweet chocolate, chopped
    - 1 tablespoon unsalted butter

Instructions:

1. **Make the churro dough**: In a saucepan, bring water, butter, sugar, and salt to a boil. Stir in the flour until a dough forms. Remove from heat and let cool for a few minutes. Beat in the eggs and vanilla extract until smooth.
2. **Fry the churros**: Heat vegetable oil in a deep pan or fryer to 375°F (190°C). Transfer the dough to a piping bag with a star tip. Pipe 4-6-inch strips of dough into the hot oil and fry until golden brown, about 2-3 minutes. Remove and drain on paper towels.
3. **Coat in cinnamon sugar**: Combine sugar and cinnamon in a shallow dish. Roll the warm churros in the sugar mixture.
4. **Make the chocolate sauce**: In a small saucepan, heat the cream over medium heat until it begins to simmer. Pour the hot cream over the chopped chocolate and butter in a bowl. Stir until smooth and glossy.
5. **Serve**: Serve the churros with the warm chocolate sauce for dipping.

Vanilla Bean Panna Cotta

Ingredients:

- 2 cups heavy cream
- 1 cup whole milk
- 1/2 cup granulated sugar
- 1 vanilla bean, split and scraped (or 2 teaspoons vanilla extract)
- 2 teaspoons unflavored gelatin
- 3 tablespoons cold water

Instructions:

1. **Bloom the gelatin**: In a small bowl, sprinkle the gelatin over the cold water and let it sit for 5 minutes to bloom.
2. **Prepare the cream mixture**: In a saucepan, heat the heavy cream, milk, and sugar over medium heat. Add the vanilla bean seeds and pod (or vanilla extract) and bring to a simmer. Remove from heat.
3. **Combine**: Stir the bloomed gelatin into the warm cream mixture until dissolved. Remove the vanilla bean pod (if using).
4. **Chill**: Pour the mixture into individual ramekins or glasses and refrigerate for at least 4 hours, or until set.
5. **Serve**: Serve the panna cotta as is or with fresh berries or a berry compote.

Lemon Blueberry Pound Cake

Ingredients:

- 1 1/2 cups all-purpose flour
- 1 teaspoon baking powder
- 1/4 teaspoon salt
- 1/2 cup unsalted butter, softened
- 1 cup granulated sugar
- 3 large eggs
- 1 teaspoon vanilla extract
- 1 tablespoon lemon zest
- 2 tablespoons lemon juice
- 1/2 cup sour cream
- 1/2 cup fresh blueberries

Instructions:

1. **Prepare the batter**: Preheat the oven to 350°F (175°C). Grease and flour a loaf pan. In a bowl, whisk together flour, baking powder, and salt. In another bowl, beat together butter and sugar until light and fluffy. Add the eggs, one at a time, followed by vanilla, lemon zest, and lemon juice.
2. **Mix the dry ingredients**: Gradually add the flour mixture to the wet ingredients, alternating with sour cream, until combined. Gently fold in the blueberries.
3. **Bake**: Pour the batter into the prepared pan and bake for 55-60 minutes, or until a toothpick inserted into the center comes out clean. Let cool in the pan for 10 minutes, then transfer to a wire rack to cool completely.

Chocolate Soufflé

Ingredients:

- 1/2 cup heavy cream
- 1/2 cup whole milk
- 4 oz semi-sweet chocolate, chopped
- 3 large eggs, separated
- 1/4 cup granulated sugar
- 1 teaspoon vanilla extract
- Pinch of salt
- Butter (for greasing ramekins)
- Powdered sugar (for dusting)

Instructions:

1. **Prepare the chocolate mixture**: In a saucepan, heat the heavy cream and milk over medium heat until just simmering. Remove from heat and stir in the chocolate until smooth. Let cool slightly.
2. **Make the soufflé base**: Whisk the egg yolks and sugar until pale. Stir in the chocolate mixture and vanilla extract.
3. **Beat the egg whites**: In a separate bowl, beat the egg whites with a pinch of salt until stiff peaks form.
4. **Fold together**: Gently fold the egg whites into the chocolate mixture until just combined.
5. **Bake**: Preheat the oven to 375°F (190°C). Butter 4 ramekins and divide the soufflé mixture between them. Bake for 12-15 minutes, or until puffed and set. Dust with powdered sugar before serving.

Crème Brûlée

Ingredients:

- 2 cups heavy cream
- 1 vanilla bean, split and scraped (or 2 teaspoons vanilla extract)
- 5 large egg yolks
- 1/2 cup granulated sugar
- 1/4 cup light brown sugar

Instructions:

1. **Prepare the cream mixture**: In a saucepan, heat the heavy cream and vanilla bean (or extract) over medium heat until just simmering. Remove from heat and let steep for 10 minutes. Remove the vanilla bean pod if using.
2. **Mix egg yolks and sugar**: In a bowl, whisk the egg yolks and granulated sugar until pale and smooth.
3. **Combine**: Gradually pour the warm cream mixture into the egg yolks, stirring constantly to temper the eggs.
4. **Bake**: Preheat the oven to 325°F (165°C). Pour the custard into ramekins and place them in a baking dish. Add hot water to the dish, halfway up the sides of the ramekins. Bake for 35-40 minutes, or until the custard is set but still jiggly in the center.
5. **Chill**: Refrigerate for at least 2 hours before serving.
6. **Caramelize the sugar**: Just before serving, sprinkle a thin layer of brown sugar on top of each custard and use a kitchen torch to caramelize the sugar until golden and crisp.

Black Forest Cake

Ingredients:

- **For the cake:**
    - 2 cups all-purpose flour
    - 1 1/2 teaspoons baking powder
    - 1/2 teaspoon salt
    - 1/2 cup unsweetened cocoa powder
    - 1 cup granulated sugar
    - 2 large eggs
    - 1 teaspoon vanilla extract
    - 1 cup buttermilk
    - 1/2 cup vegetable oil
    - 1/2 cup boiling water
- **For the filling:**
    - 2 cups heavy whipping cream
    - 2 tablespoons powdered sugar
    - 1 teaspoon vanilla extract
    - 1 jar (24 oz) morello cherries, drained
    - 2 tablespoons cherry juice

Instructions:

1. **Make the cake**: Preheat the oven to 350°F (175°C). Grease and flour two 9-inch round cake pans. In a bowl, whisk together flour, baking powder, salt, cocoa powder, and sugar. In another bowl, whisk the eggs, vanilla, buttermilk, and oil. Gradually add the wet ingredients to the dry, then add boiling water and mix until smooth.
2. **Bake the cake**: Divide the batter between the prepared pans and bake for 25-30 minutes. Let the cakes cool in the pans for 10 minutes before transferring to a wire rack.
3. **Make the whipped cream**: In a mixing bowl, whip the heavy cream with powdered sugar and vanilla until stiff peaks form.
4. **Assemble the cake**: Slice the cakes in half horizontally. Layer with whipped cream, cherries, and some cherry juice. Frost the top with the remaining whipped cream and top with more cherries.

Mocha Trifle

Ingredients:

- 2 cups brewed coffee, cooled
- 1 tablespoon coffee liqueur (optional)
- 1 package (15 oz) chocolate cake mix (or homemade cake)
- 2 cups whipped cream
- 1 cup mascarpone cheese, softened
- 1/4 cup powdered sugar
- 2 tablespoons cocoa powder
- 1/2 cup chocolate shavings

Instructions:

1. **Make the cake**: Prepare the chocolate cake mix according to package instructions and let it cool. Cut the cake into cubes.
2. **Make the cream mixture**: In a bowl, whisk together mascarpone cheese, powdered sugar, and cocoa powder until smooth. Fold in whipped cream until well combined.
3. **Assemble the trifle**: In a large trifle dish, layer the cake cubes with coffee-soaked cake, cream mixture, and chocolate shavings. Repeat layers and top with more whipped cream and chocolate shavings.
4. **Chill**: Refrigerate for at least 4 hours before serving to allow flavors to meld.

Vanilla Almond Cake

Ingredients:

- 2 cups all-purpose flour
- 1 1/2 teaspoons baking powder
- 1/2 teaspoon salt
- 1/2 cup unsalted butter, softened
- 1 cup granulated sugar
- 2 large eggs
- 1 teaspoon vanilla extract
- 1 teaspoon almond extract
- 1 cup whole milk

For the frosting:

- 1/2 cup unsalted butter, softened
- 2 cups powdered sugar
- 1 teaspoon vanilla extract
- 2 tablespoons heavy cream
- 1/4 teaspoon almond extract

Instructions:

1. **Make the cake**: Preheat the oven to 350°F (175°C). Grease and flour two 9-inch round cake pans. In a bowl, whisk together flour, baking powder, and salt. In another bowl, cream together butter and sugar until light and fluffy. Add the eggs, one at a time, followed by vanilla and almond extracts. Alternate adding the dry ingredients and milk, beginning and ending with the dry ingredients.
2. **Bake**: Pour the batter evenly into the prepared pans and bake for 25-30 minutes, or until a toothpick inserted comes out clean. Let the cakes cool in the pans for 10 minutes before transferring to a wire rack.
3. **Make the frosting**: Beat the butter until creamy, then gradually add powdered sugar, vanilla, almond extract, and heavy cream. Frost the cooled cake.

Raspberry Almond Tart

Ingredients:

- **For the crust:**
    - 1 1/2 cups all-purpose flour
    - 1/4 cup powdered sugar
    - 1/2 teaspoon salt
    - 1/2 cup unsalted butter, cubed
    - 1 egg yolk
    - 2-3 tablespoons cold water
- **For the filling:**
    - 1/2 cup almond meal
    - 1/4 cup granulated sugar
    - 1/4 cup unsalted butter, softened
    - 1 large egg
    - 1 teaspoon vanilla extract
    - 1/4 cup raspberry jam
    - 1/2 cup fresh raspberries

Instructions:

1. **Make the crust**: Preheat the oven to 375°F (190°C). In a food processor, combine flour, powdered sugar, and salt. Add butter and pulse until the mixture resembles coarse crumbs. Add the egg yolk and cold water, pulsing until the dough comes together. Press into a tart pan and bake for 10-12 minutes, or until golden.
2. **Make the filling**: In a bowl, cream together almond meal, sugar, butter, egg, and vanilla until smooth. Spread a thin layer of raspberry jam over the cooled tart shell. Pour the almond filling on top and smooth into an even layer.
3. **Bake**: Bake for 20-25 minutes, or until the filling is golden and set. Let cool before topping with fresh raspberries.

Peanut Butter Chocolate Pie

Ingredients:

- **For the crust:**
    - 1 1/2 cups chocolate wafer crumbs
    - 1/4 cup granulated sugar
    - 1/4 cup unsalted butter, melted
- **For the filling:**
    - 1 cup creamy peanut butter
    - 1/2 cup powdered sugar
    - 8 oz cream cheese, softened
    - 1 cup heavy cream
    - 1 teaspoon vanilla extract
- **For the topping:**
    - 1/2 cup semi-sweet chocolate chips
    - 2 tablespoons heavy cream

Instructions:

1. **Make the crust**: Preheat the oven to 350°F (175°C). In a bowl, mix together the chocolate wafer crumbs, sugar, and melted butter. Press the mixture into the bottom of a pie dish and bake for 10 minutes. Let cool.
2. **Make the filling**: In a large bowl, beat together peanut butter, powdered sugar, and cream cheese until smooth. In a separate bowl, whip the heavy cream and vanilla until stiff peaks form. Fold the whipped cream into the peanut butter mixture until fully combined. Pour the filling into the cooled crust.
3. **Make the topping**: In a microwave-safe bowl, melt the chocolate chips with heavy cream in 20-second intervals, stirring in between, until smooth. Drizzle the chocolate over the peanut butter filling.
4. **Chill**: Refrigerate the pie for at least 4 hours, or until firm.

Pecan Praline Cheesecake

Ingredients:

- **For the crust:**
    - 1 1/2 cups graham cracker crumbs
    - 1/4 cup granulated sugar
    - 1/2 teaspoon ground cinnamon
    - 1/4 cup unsalted butter, melted
- **For the filling:**
    - 3 cups cream cheese, softened
    - 1 cup granulated sugar
    - 3 large eggs
    - 1 teaspoon vanilla extract
    - 1/2 cup sour cream
    - 1/4 cup all-purpose flour
- **For the pecan praline topping:**
    - 1/2 cup unsalted butter
    - 1 cup brown sugar, packed
    - 1/4 cup heavy cream
    - 1 1/2 cups chopped pecans

Instructions:

1. **Make the crust**: Preheat the oven to 325°F (165°C). In a bowl, combine the graham cracker crumbs, sugar, cinnamon, and melted butter. Press the mixture into the bottom of a 9-inch springform pan. Bake for 10 minutes, then let cool.
2. **Make the filling**: Beat the cream cheese and sugar until smooth. Add the eggs one at a time, mixing well after each addition. Stir in the vanilla, sour cream, and flour. Pour the mixture into the crust and bake for 55-60 minutes, or until the center is set. Let cool.
3. **Make the praline topping**: In a saucepan, melt the butter and brown sugar over medium heat. Stir in the heavy cream and bring to a simmer. Cook for 2-3 minutes until thickened. Remove from heat and stir in the pecans.
4. **Top the cheesecake**: Pour the pecan praline mixture over the cooled cheesecake and refrigerate for at least 4 hours before serving.

Banana Foster Cake

Ingredients:

- **For the cake:**
    - 1 1/2 cups all-purpose flour
    - 1 teaspoon baking soda
    - 1/2 teaspoon salt
    - 1/2 teaspoon ground cinnamon
    - 1/2 cup unsalted butter, softened
    - 1 cup granulated sugar
    - 2 large eggs
    - 1 teaspoon vanilla extract
    - 3 ripe bananas, mashed
    - 1/2 cup buttermilk
- **For the sauce:**
    - 1/4 cup unsalted butter
    - 1/4 cup brown sugar, packed
    - 2 tablespoons dark rum
    - 1/2 teaspoon cinnamon
    - 1 banana, sliced

Instructions:

1. **Make the cake**: Preheat the oven to 350°F (175°C). Grease and flour a 9-inch round cake pan. In a bowl, whisk together flour, baking soda, salt, and cinnamon. In another bowl, cream the butter and sugar until light and fluffy. Add the eggs one at a time, then stir in the vanilla, mashed bananas, and buttermilk. Gradually add the dry ingredients and mix until just combined. Pour into the prepared pan and bake for 25-30 minutes, or until a toothpick comes out clean.
2. **Make the sauce**: In a saucepan, melt the butter and brown sugar over medium heat. Stir in the rum and cinnamon, then cook for 1-2 minutes. Add the banana slices and cook for another minute until softened.
3. **Serve**: Slice the cake and drizzle with the banana foster sauce.

Key Lime Pie

Ingredients:

- **For the crust:**
  - 1 1/2 cups graham cracker crumbs
  - 1/4 cup granulated sugar
  - 1/4 cup unsalted butter, melted
- **For the filling:**
  - 3 large egg yolks
  - 1 can (14 oz) sweetened condensed milk
  - 1/2 cup fresh key lime juice
  - 1 tablespoon lime zest
- **For the topping:**
  - 1 cup heavy cream
  - 2 tablespoons powdered sugar
  - 1 teaspoon vanilla extract

Instructions:

1. **Make the crust**: Preheat the oven to 350°F (175°C). Combine the graham cracker crumbs, sugar, and melted butter in a bowl. Press into the bottom of a pie dish and bake for 10 minutes. Let cool.
2. **Make the filling**: Whisk the egg yolks in a bowl. Add the sweetened condensed milk, lime juice, and lime zest, and whisk until smooth. Pour the filling into the cooled crust and bake for 15-18 minutes. Let cool, then refrigerate for at least 4 hours.
3. **Make the topping**: Whip the heavy cream with powdered sugar and vanilla until stiff peaks form. Spread over the chilled pie.

Coffee Hazelnut Torte

Ingredients:

- **For the cake:**
    - 1 cup hazelnut flour
    - 1/2 cup all-purpose flour
    - 1/2 teaspoon baking powder
    - 1/2 teaspoon baking soda
    - 1/2 cup unsalted butter, softened
    - 1/2 cup granulated sugar
    - 2 large eggs
    - 1 teaspoon vanilla extract
    - 1/2 cup brewed coffee, cooled
- **For the frosting:**
    - 1/2 cup unsalted butter, softened
    - 1/4 cup powdered sugar
    - 1/2 cup coffee-flavored liqueur
    - 1/4 cup cocoa powder
    - 1/2 cup heavy cream

Instructions:

1. **Make the cake**: Preheat the oven to 350°F (175°C). Grease and flour two 8-inch cake pans. In a bowl, whisk together hazelnut flour, all-purpose flour, baking powder, and baking soda. In another bowl, cream the butter and sugar until fluffy. Add the eggs, one at a time, followed by the vanilla. Gradually add the dry ingredients and brewed coffee, mixing until smooth. Bake for 20-25 minutes, then cool.
2. **Make the frosting**: Beat the butter, powdered sugar, coffee liqueur, cocoa powder, and heavy cream until smooth. Frost the cooled cakes.

Strawberry Shortcake

Ingredients:

- **For the shortcakes:**
    - 2 cups all-purpose flour
    - 1/4 cup granulated sugar
    - 2 teaspoons baking powder
    - 1/2 teaspoon salt
    - 1/2 cup unsalted butter, cold and cubed
    - 2/3 cup heavy cream
    - 1 teaspoon vanilla extract
- **For the topping:**
    - 2 cups fresh strawberries, hulled and sliced
    - 1/4 cup granulated sugar
    - 1 cup heavy cream
    - 2 tablespoons powdered sugar
    - 1 teaspoon vanilla extract

Instructions:

1. **Make the shortcakes**: Preheat the oven to 400°F (200°C). In a bowl, whisk together flour, sugar, baking powder, and salt. Cut in the butter until the mixture resembles coarse crumbs. Stir in the heavy cream and vanilla until just combined. Drop spoonfuls of the dough onto a baking sheet and bake for 12-15 minutes, or until golden brown. Let cool.
2. **Prepare the topping**: Toss the strawberries with sugar and let sit for 15 minutes. Whip the heavy cream with powdered sugar and vanilla until stiff peaks form.
3. **Assemble the shortcakes**: Slice the shortcakes in half, top with strawberries and whipped cream, and serve.

Chocolate Dipped Strawberries

Ingredients:

- 1 lb fresh strawberries, hulled
- 8 oz semi-sweet chocolate chips
- 4 oz white chocolate chips (optional for drizzling)

Instructions:

1. **Prepare the strawberries**: Wash and dry the strawberries thoroughly, leaving the stems on.
2. **Melt the chocolate**: In a microwave-safe bowl, melt the semi-sweet chocolate chips in 30-second intervals, stirring between each, until smooth.
3. **Dip the strawberries**: Hold each strawberry by the stem and dip it into the melted chocolate. Let the excess drip off, then place on a parchment-lined baking sheet.
4. **Optional drizzle**: Melt the white chocolate chips in the same way, and drizzle over the dipped strawberries. Refrigerate for 30 minutes to set the chocolate.

Mango Sorbet

Ingredients:

- 3 ripe mangoes, peeled and chopped
- 1/2 cup water
- 1/2 cup sugar
- 1 tablespoon fresh lime juice
- 1/4 teaspoon salt

Instructions:

1. **Make the syrup**: In a small saucepan, combine water and sugar. Heat over medium heat, stirring until the sugar dissolves. Remove from heat and let cool.
2. **Blend the mango**: In a blender, combine the mangoes, lime juice, salt, and cooled syrup. Blend until smooth.
3. **Chill and churn**: Pour the mango mixture into an ice cream maker and churn according to the manufacturer's instructions. Once the sorbet reaches the desired consistency, transfer it to a container and freeze for at least 2 hours before serving.

Carrot Cake with Cream Cheese Frosting

Ingredients:

- **For the cake:**
    - 2 cups all-purpose flour
    - 1 1/2 teaspoons baking powder
    - 1/2 teaspoon baking soda
    - 1 teaspoon cinnamon
    - 1/2 teaspoon salt
    - 1 1/2 cups vegetable oil
    - 1 1/2 cups granulated sugar
    - 4 large eggs
    - 2 teaspoons vanilla extract
    - 2 cups finely grated carrots
    - 1/2 cup chopped walnuts or pecans (optional)
- **For the frosting:**
    - 8 oz cream cheese, softened
    - 1/2 cup unsalted butter, softened
    - 4 cups powdered sugar
    - 1 teaspoon vanilla extract

Instructions:

1. **Make the cake**: Preheat the oven to 350°F (175°C). Grease and flour two 9-inch round cake pans. In a bowl, whisk together flour, baking powder, baking soda, cinnamon, and salt. In a separate bowl, beat the oil, sugar, eggs, and vanilla until smooth. Gradually add the dry ingredients, mixing until just combined. Stir in the grated carrots and nuts (if using). Pour the batter into the prepared pans and bake for 30-35 minutes or until a toothpick comes out clean. Let cool completely.
2. **Make the frosting**: Beat the cream cheese and butter until smooth. Gradually add the powdered sugar and vanilla, and beat until fluffy. Frost the cooled cakes.

Chocolate Coconut Macaroons

Ingredients:

- 2 1/2 cups sweetened shredded coconut
- 1/4 cup cocoa powder
- 1/4 teaspoon salt
- 3 large egg whites
- 1/2 cup granulated sugar
- 1 teaspoon vanilla extract
- 4 oz semi-sweet chocolate chips (optional for dipping)

Instructions:

1. Preheat the oven to 325°F (163°C). Line a baking sheet with parchment paper.
2. In a large bowl, mix the coconut, cocoa powder, and salt. In a separate bowl, beat the egg whites and sugar until stiff peaks form. Gently fold the egg whites into the coconut mixture.
3. Using a spoon, scoop out the mixture and form into mounds on the prepared baking sheet. Bake for 15-20 minutes or until golden brown.
4. Optional: Melt the chocolate chips in a microwave-safe bowl and dip the cooled macaroons in the chocolate, then place them back on the parchment paper to set.

S'mores Bars

Ingredients:

- 1 cup graham cracker crumbs
- 1/4 cup unsalted butter, melted
- 1 cup mini marshmallows
- 1 cup chocolate chips
- 1/2 cup sweetened condensed milk

Instructions:

1. Preheat the oven to 350°F (175°C). Line an 8x8-inch baking dish with parchment paper.
2. Mix the graham cracker crumbs and melted butter in a bowl, then press into the bottom of the prepared dish. Bake for 8-10 minutes.
3. Remove from the oven and top with mini marshmallows, chocolate chips, and drizzle with sweetened condensed milk. Return to the oven and bake for an additional 5-7 minutes, until the marshmallows are golden. Let cool before cutting into bars.

Coconut Cream Pie

Ingredients:

- **For the crust:**
    - 1 1/2 cups graham cracker crumbs
    - 1/4 cup granulated sugar
    - 1/4 cup unsalted butter, melted
- **For the filling:**
    - 2 cups whole milk
    - 1 cup heavy cream
    - 1/2 cup granulated sugar
    - 1/4 cup cornstarch
    - 1/4 teaspoon salt
    - 4 large egg yolks
    - 1 teaspoon vanilla extract
    - 1 1/2 cups shredded coconut (unsweetened)
    - 1/2 cup whipped cream (for topping)

Instructions:

1. **Make the crust**: Preheat the oven to 350°F (175°C). Combine the graham cracker crumbs, sugar, and melted butter in a bowl. Press the mixture into the bottom of a pie dish and bake for 10 minutes. Let cool.
2. **Make the filling**: In a saucepan, combine the milk, cream, sugar, cornstarch, and salt. Cook over medium heat, whisking constantly until thickened. In a separate bowl, whisk the egg yolks, then gradually whisk in some of the hot milk mixture to temper the eggs. Return everything to the pan and cook for another 2 minutes. Remove from heat and stir in vanilla and coconut. Pour the filling into the cooled crust. Chill for 4 hours. Top with whipped cream before serving.

Brown Butter Chocolate Chip Cookies

Ingredients:

- 1 cup unsalted butter
- 1 cup granulated sugar
- 1/2 cup packed brown sugar
- 2 teaspoons vanilla extract
- 2 large eggs
- 2 1/2 cups all-purpose flour
- 1 teaspoon baking soda
- 1/2 teaspoon salt
- 2 cups chocolate chips

Instructions:

1. **Brown the butter**: In a saucepan, melt the butter over medium heat. Continue to cook, swirling the pan occasionally, until the butter turns golden brown and smells nutty. Remove from heat and let cool slightly.
2. **Make the dough**: Preheat the oven to 350°F (175°C). In a bowl, beat the browned butter, sugars, and vanilla until smooth. Add the eggs, one at a time, beating well after each. Gradually add the flour, baking soda, and salt. Stir in the chocolate chips.
3. Drop spoonfuls of dough onto a baking sheet and bake for 8-10 minutes, or until the edges are golden. Let cool on a wire rack.

Pumpkin Cheesecake

Ingredients:

- **For the crust:**
    - 1 1/2 cups graham cracker crumbs
    - 1/4 cup sugar
    - 1/2 cup unsalted butter, melted
- **For the filling:**
    - 3 packages (8 oz each) cream cheese, softened
    - 1 cup granulated sugar
    - 3 large eggs
    - 1 can (15 oz) pure pumpkin
    - 1 teaspoon vanilla extract
    - 1 teaspoon cinnamon
    - 1/2 teaspoon ground ginger
    - 1/4 teaspoon ground cloves

Instructions:

1. **Make the crust**: Preheat the oven to 325°F (165°C). Mix the graham cracker crumbs, sugar, and melted butter, then press into the bottom of a springform pan. Bake for 10 minutes and let cool.
2. **Make the filling**: In a bowl, beat the cream cheese and sugar until smooth. Add the eggs, one at a time, beating after each. Stir in the pumpkin, vanilla, cinnamon, ginger, and cloves. Pour into the cooled crust.
3. Bake for 55-60 minutes, or until the center is set. Let cool before chilling in the fridge for at least 4 hours before serving.

Chilled Lemon Pudding

Ingredients:

- 2 cups whole milk
- 1/2 cup granulated sugar
- 1/4 cup cornstarch
- 1/4 teaspoon salt
- 3 large egg yolks
- 2 tablespoons unsalted butter
- 2 teaspoons lemon zest
- 1/4 cup fresh lemon juice

Instructions:

1. In a saucepan, combine milk, sugar, cornstarch, and salt. Cook over medium heat, whisking constantly until thickened.
2. In a bowl, whisk the egg yolks. Gradually add some of the hot milk mixture to the yolks to temper them. Pour everything back into the pan and cook for another 2 minutes.
3. Remove from heat, stir in butter, lemon zest, and juice. Pour into individual serving dishes and refrigerate for at least 2 hours before serving.

Triple Chocolate Mousse

Ingredients:

- 4 oz dark chocolate, chopped
- 4 oz milk chocolate, chopped
- 4 oz white chocolate, chopped
- 1 1/2 cups heavy cream
- 1 tablespoon powdered sugar
- 1 teaspoon vanilla extract

Instructions:

1. **Melt the chocolate**: In three separate bowls, melt the dark, milk, and white chocolate over a double boiler or in the microwave in short bursts. Let cool slightly.
2. **Whip the cream**: In a bowl, beat the heavy cream with powdered sugar and vanilla until stiff peaks form.
3. **Make the mousse**: Fold the whipped cream into each type of melted chocolate, one at a time, creating three separate mousse mixtures.
4. Spoon the mousses into serving glasses, layering them for a triple-chocolate effect. Chill for at least 2 hours before serving.

Cherry Clafoutis

Ingredients:

- 2 cups fresh cherries, pitted
- 1 cup whole milk
- 1/2 cup all-purpose flour
- 1/4 cup granulated sugar
- 3 large eggs
- 1 teaspoon vanilla extract
- 1/4 teaspoon salt
- Powdered sugar, for dusting

Instructions:

1. Preheat the oven to 375°F (190°C) and grease a 9-inch round baking dish.
2. Arrange the pitted cherries in the bottom of the baking dish.
3. In a bowl, whisk together milk, flour, sugar, eggs, vanilla, and salt until smooth. Pour the batter over the cherries.
4. Bake for 35-40 minutes or until golden brown and puffed up.
5. Allow to cool slightly before dusting with powdered sugar and serving.

Strawberry Rhubarb Galette

Ingredients:

- **For the dough:**
    - 1 1/2 cups all-purpose flour
    - 1/4 cup sugar
    - 1/2 teaspoon salt
    - 1/2 cup cold unsalted butter, cubed
    - 1/4 cup ice water
- **For the filling:**
    - 1 cup fresh strawberries, sliced
    - 1 cup fresh rhubarb, chopped
    - 1/2 cup sugar
    - 1 tablespoon cornstarch
    - 1 teaspoon vanilla extract
    - 1 tablespoon lemon juice

Instructions:

1. **Make the dough**: In a food processor, pulse together flour, sugar, and salt. Add butter and pulse until the mixture resembles coarse crumbs. Add ice water and pulse until the dough just comes together. Form into a disk, wrap in plastic wrap, and refrigerate for 30 minutes.
2. **Prepare the filling**: In a bowl, combine the strawberries, rhubarb, sugar, cornstarch, vanilla, and lemon juice.
3. **Assemble the galette**: Preheat the oven to 375°F (190°C). Roll out the dough on a floured surface to a 12-inch circle. Place the filling in the center, leaving a border around the edges. Fold the edges over the filling to form a rustic crust.
4. Bake for 40-45 minutes, until the crust is golden and the filling is bubbling. Let cool before slicing.

Ice Cream Sandwiches

Ingredients:

- **For the cookies:**
    - 1 cup unsalted butter, softened
    - 3/4 cup granulated sugar
    - 3/4 cup brown sugar, packed
    - 2 large eggs
    - 1 teaspoon vanilla extract
    - 2 1/4 cups all-purpose flour
    - 1 teaspoon baking soda
    - 1/2 teaspoon salt
    - 1 cup chocolate chips
- **For the filling:**
    - 1 quart vanilla ice cream

Instructions:

1. **Make the cookies**: Preheat the oven to 350°F (175°C). Line two baking sheets with parchment paper.
2. In a bowl, cream together butter, granulated sugar, and brown sugar until light and fluffy. Add eggs and vanilla, and beat until combined.
3. Gradually add flour, baking soda, and salt. Stir in the chocolate chips.
4. Scoop dough onto baking sheets, spacing about 2 inches apart. Bake for 10-12 minutes until golden. Let cool completely.
5. **Assemble the sandwiches**: Scoop a generous amount of vanilla ice cream onto the bottom of one cookie, then top with another cookie. Press gently to spread the ice cream evenly. Repeat for the remaining cookies. Freeze until firm, about 30 minutes.

Blueberry Lemon Cheesecake Bars

Ingredients:

- **For the crust:**
    - 1 1/2 cups graham cracker crumbs
    - 1/4 cup granulated sugar
    - 1/2 cup unsalted butter, melted
- **For the filling:**
    - 2 packages (8 oz each) cream cheese, softened
    - 1 cup granulated sugar
    - 3 large eggs
    - 1/4 cup fresh lemon juice
    - 1 tablespoon lemon zest
    - 1 teaspoon vanilla extract
    - 1 cup fresh blueberries

Instructions:

1. **Make the crust**: Preheat the oven to 325°F (165°C). Mix graham cracker crumbs, sugar, and melted butter in a bowl. Press the mixture into the bottom of a greased 9x13-inch baking dish. Bake for 10 minutes.
2. **Make the filling**: In a bowl, beat cream cheese and sugar until smooth. Add eggs, lemon juice, lemon zest, and vanilla, and mix until combined.
3. Fold in the blueberries gently. Pour the mixture over the crust and smooth the top.
4. Bake for 30-35 minutes, until the center is set. Let cool completely, then refrigerate for at least 4 hours before cutting into bars.

Matcha Green Tea Cookies

Ingredients:

- 2 cups all-purpose flour
- 1 tablespoon matcha green tea powder
- 1/2 teaspoon baking soda
- 1/4 teaspoon salt
- 1/2 cup unsalted butter, softened
- 1 cup granulated sugar
- 1 large egg
- 1 teaspoon vanilla extract

Instructions:

1. Preheat the oven to 350°F (175°C). Line a baking sheet with parchment paper.
2. In a bowl, whisk together flour, matcha powder, baking soda, and salt.
3. In a separate bowl, cream together butter and sugar until light and fluffy. Add the egg and vanilla, and mix well.
4. Gradually add the dry ingredients and stir until combined.
5. Scoop dough into tablespoon-sized balls and place on the prepared baking sheet. Bake for 10-12 minutes until edges are golden. Let cool before serving.

Cinnamon Roll Apple Pie

Ingredients:

- **For the crust:**
    - 1 package refrigerated cinnamon rolls (8 rolls)
    - 2 tablespoons unsalted butter, melted
- **For the filling:**
    - 4 cups peeled and sliced apples
    - 1/2 cup granulated sugar
    - 1 teaspoon ground cinnamon
    - 1 tablespoon cornstarch
    - 1 tablespoon lemon juice

Instructions:

1. Preheat the oven to 375°F (190°C). Grease a 9-inch pie dish.
2. Unroll the cinnamon rolls and arrange them around the edges of the pie dish to form a crust. Brush with melted butter.
3. In a bowl, combine apples, sugar, cinnamon, cornstarch, and lemon juice. Pour the mixture into the cinnamon roll crust.
4. Bake for 35-40 minutes, until the apples are tender and the crust is golden. Let cool before serving.

Coconut Rice Pudding

Ingredients:

- 1 cup Arborio rice
- 2 cups coconut milk
- 1 1/2 cups whole milk
- 1/4 cup sugar
- 1 teaspoon vanilla extract
- 1/4 teaspoon ground cinnamon (optional)

Instructions:

1. In a large saucepan, combine the rice, coconut milk, whole milk, and sugar. Cook over medium heat, stirring occasionally, until the mixture comes to a simmer.
2. Reduce the heat to low and cook for 20-25 minutes, stirring frequently, until the rice is tender and the pudding thickens.
3. Stir in the vanilla extract and cinnamon (if using). Serve warm or chilled.

Chocolate Hazelnut Truffles

Ingredients:

- 8 oz semi-sweet chocolate, chopped
- 1/2 cup heavy cream
- 2 tablespoons unsalted butter
- 1/4 cup hazelnut spread (like Nutella)
- Cocoa powder or crushed hazelnuts for coating

Instructions:

1. In a saucepan, heat the cream and butter until warm, but not boiling. Pour over the chopped chocolate and stir until smooth.
2. Stir in the hazelnut spread until well combined. Let the mixture cool, then refrigerate for 1-2 hours until firm.
3. Roll the chilled chocolate mixture into small balls, then coat in cocoa powder or crushed hazelnuts. Store in the refrigerator.

Cherry Almond Cake

Ingredients:

- 1 1/2 cups all-purpose flour
- 1 teaspoon baking powder
- 1/2 teaspoon salt
- 1/2 cup unsalted butter, softened
- 1 cup granulated sugar
- 2 large eggs
- 1 teaspoon vanilla extract
- 1/4 teaspoon almond extract
- 1/2 cup milk
- 1 cup fresh cherries, pitted and chopped
- 1/4 cup sliced almonds

Instructions:

1. Preheat the oven to 350°F (175°C). Grease and flour a 9-inch round cake pan.
2. In a bowl, whisk together flour, baking powder, and salt.
3. In a separate bowl, cream together butter and sugar until light and fluffy. Add the eggs, vanilla extract, and almond extract, and mix until smooth.
4. Gradually add the flour mixture and milk, alternating between the two. Fold in the cherries.
5. Pour the batter into the prepared pan and sprinkle with almonds.
6. Bake for 35-40 minutes or until a toothpick comes out clean. Let cool before serving.

Lemon Coconut Bars

Ingredients:

- **For the crust:**
    - 1 1/2 cups all-purpose flour
    - 1/2 cup unsweetened shredded coconut
    - 1/4 cup powdered sugar
    - 1/2 cup unsalted butter, softened
- **For the filling:**
    - 3 large eggs
    - 1 cup granulated sugar
    - 1/2 cup fresh lemon juice
    - 1 tablespoon lemon zest
    - 1/4 cup all-purpose flour
    - 1/2 teaspoon baking powder
    - 1/4 teaspoon salt
    - 1/4 cup unsweetened shredded coconut

Instructions:

1. **Make the crust**: Preheat the oven to 350°F (175°C). Grease a 9-inch square baking dish.
2. In a bowl, combine flour, shredded coconut, powdered sugar, and melted butter. Press the mixture into the bottom of the prepared baking dish.
3. Bake for 15 minutes until lightly golden.
4. **Make the filling**: In a separate bowl, whisk together eggs, sugar, lemon juice, lemon zest, flour, baking powder, and salt. Fold in the shredded coconut.
5. Pour the filling over the baked crust and bake for another 20-25 minutes until set and golden.
6. Allow to cool completely before cutting into bars. Dust with powdered sugar before serving.

Flourless Chocolate Cake

Ingredients:

- 1 cup unsalted butter
- 8 oz semi-sweet chocolate, chopped
- 1 cup granulated sugar
- 1/4 teaspoon salt
- 1 teaspoon vanilla extract
- 4 large eggs, at room temperature
- 1/2 cup unsweetened cocoa powder
- Powdered sugar, for dusting

Instructions:

1. Preheat the oven to 375°F (190°C). Grease a 9-inch round cake pan and line the bottom with parchment paper.
2. In a saucepan, melt butter and chocolate together over low heat, stirring until smooth. Remove from heat and stir in sugar, salt, and vanilla extract.
3. Whisk in eggs one at a time until well combined. Stir in cocoa powder until smooth.
4. Pour the batter into the prepared cake pan and bake for 20-25 minutes, or until the cake is set but still slightly soft in the center.
5. Let the cake cool completely in the pan before inverting onto a serving platter. Dust with powdered sugar and serve.

Almond Joy Cheesecake

Ingredients:

- **For the crust:**
    - 1 1/2 cups graham cracker crumbs
    - 1/4 cup unsweetened cocoa powder
    - 1/4 cup granulated sugar
    - 1/2 cup unsalted butter, melted
- **For the cheesecake filling:**
    - 3 packages (8 oz each) cream cheese, softened
    - 1 cup granulated sugar
    - 1 teaspoon vanilla extract
    - 3 large eggs
    - 1 cup sour cream
    - 1/2 cup shredded coconut
    - 1/2 cup chopped almonds
    - 1/2 cup chocolate chips

Instructions:

1. **Make the crust**: Preheat the oven to 325°F (165°C). Grease a 9-inch springform pan.
2. In a bowl, combine graham cracker crumbs, cocoa powder, sugar, and melted butter. Press the mixture into the bottom of the pan. Bake for 10 minutes, then remove and set aside.
3. **Make the filling**: In a large bowl, beat the cream cheese and sugar until smooth. Add vanilla extract, eggs, and sour cream, and beat until combined.
4. Fold in shredded coconut, chopped almonds, and chocolate chips.
5. Pour the mixture over the crust and bake for 50-60 minutes, until the center is set.
6. Let the cheesecake cool completely, then refrigerate for at least 4 hours before serving.

Honey Lavender Ice Cream

Ingredients:

- 1 1/2 cups whole milk
- 1 1/2 cups heavy cream
- 1/2 cup honey
- 1 tablespoon dried lavender flowers
- 5 large egg yolks
- 1 teaspoon vanilla extract

Instructions:

1. In a saucepan, combine milk, heavy cream, honey, and lavender flowers. Heat over medium heat until the mixture just begins to simmer. Remove from heat and let steep for 10 minutes.
2. Strain the mixture to remove the lavender flowers.
3. In a bowl, whisk the egg yolks. Gradually pour in the warm milk mixture while whisking constantly.
4. Return the mixture to the saucepan and cook over low heat, stirring constantly, until it thickens enough to coat the back of a spoon.
5. Remove from heat, stir in vanilla extract, and chill the mixture for at least 4 hours.
6. Churn the mixture in an ice cream maker according to the manufacturer's instructions. Freeze until firm.

Apple Cinnamon Rolls

Ingredients:

- **For the dough:**
    - 3 1/4 cups all-purpose flour
    - 1/4 cup granulated sugar
    - 1 package active dry yeast
    - 1/2 cup whole milk
    - 1/4 cup water
    - 1/2 cup unsalted butter, softened
    - 2 large eggs
    - 1 teaspoon salt
- **For the filling:**
    - 1/2 cup unsalted butter, softened
    - 1/2 cup brown sugar, packed
    - 2 teaspoons ground cinnamon
    - 2 cups peeled and chopped apples (about 2 medium apples)
- **For the glaze:**
    - 1 cup powdered sugar
    - 2 tablespoons milk
    - 1 teaspoon vanilla extract

Instructions:

1. **Make the dough**: In a small saucepan, heat milk and water until warm. Stir in sugar and yeast. Let sit for 5 minutes to activate the yeast.
2. In a large bowl, combine flour and salt. Add the yeast mixture, butter, and eggs, and knead until a dough forms. Let the dough rise for 1 hour, or until doubled in size.
3. **Make the filling**: In a bowl, mix butter, brown sugar, and cinnamon.
4. Roll the dough into a rectangle and spread the cinnamon-sugar mixture evenly. Sprinkle with chopped apples. Roll the dough tightly and slice into 12 rolls.
5. Place the rolls in a greased 9x13-inch pan and let rise for 30 minutes.
6. Preheat the oven to 375°F (190°C) and bake for 25-30 minutes, until golden.
7. **Make the glaze**: In a bowl, whisk together powdered sugar, milk, and vanilla. Drizzle over the warm cinnamon rolls before serving.

Passion Fruit Panna Cotta

Ingredients:

- 2 cups heavy cream
- 1 cup whole milk
- 1/2 cup granulated sugar
- 1 tablespoon vanilla extract
- 1 packet (2 1/4 teaspoons) unflavored gelatin
- 1/2 cup passion fruit juice (or 2-3 passion fruits, pulp and seeds removed)

Instructions:

1. In a saucepan, combine heavy cream, milk, and sugar. Heat over medium heat until the sugar dissolves and the mixture is warm.
2. In a small bowl, sprinkle gelatin over 3 tablespoons of cold water and let it bloom for 5 minutes.
3. Stir the bloomed gelatin into the warm cream mixture until dissolved. Remove from heat and stir in vanilla extract.
4. Pour the mixture into ramekins and refrigerate for at least 4 hours or until set.
5. Once set, spoon passion fruit pulp or juice over the top and serve chilled.